Dying to Lead

The Disturbing Trend of Clergy Suicide

Lewis Brogdon

Seymour Press
Bowie, MD

Copyright © Seymour Press, 2014

All Rights Reserved

Printed in the United States of America

ISBN: 1938373049

ISBN- 13: 978- 1938373046

All Scripture is from the NIV Bible unless otherwise noted.

Table of Contents

Forward i

Dying to Lead.. 1

Pastors and the Growing Problem of Suicide 13

Helping Troubled Pastors 41

Suicide the Unpardonable Sin? 77

Prayer for Pastors, Families and Churches........... 111

Bibliography 117

Dedication

To both the families who lost husbands and fathers and to the churches who experienced the loss of their pastor to suicide. "God is our refuge and strength, a very present help in trouble." Psalm 46:1(KJV)

Forward

At a moment in history when the forces of nihilism have invaded not just mainstream society, but the sacred walls of the Church, Dr. Lewis Brogdon attends to the problem of clergy suicide, a deep and pervasive challenge to the Churches' witness in a troubled world. Swiftly emerging as a major theologian and biblical scholar of this generation, Brogdon raises very critical questions as to the nature of clergy hopelessness and despair, and why is it that the bearers of hope seem to be losing hope. By examining some contemporary cases of clergy suicide, he creates the space for urgent dialogue on the relationship between clergy and congregation, and the broader implications for clergy care, expanding to the health of congregations and communities.

The problem of clergy suicide is an issue that should raise alarms for all who are concerned with the witness of the Church, and the much broader challenge of faith amid rising Western secularization. Author of the important text,

Hope on the Brink (Cascade 2013), Brogdon introduces through this brief account an investigative appraisal on the psychological, social, cultural, and theological dimensions of a dilemma facing the Church. It speaks to the dramatic shifts taking place in clergy leadership, revealing the profound pressures facing clergy and their families, while also reflecting the reality of troubled congregations and communities. As a theologian gravely interested in the Church's witness to freedom and justice, I am grateful to Dr. Brogdon for lifting up the issue of clergy suicide, which has more often been viewed as an embarrassing internal crisis that the church, particularly denominational leadership, has been slow to respond.

What happens when the very individuals charged with preaching the Gospel of hope, peace, love, and justice, face with the most dramatic form of mental and emotional trauma? By sounding the alarm, Brogdon approaches this quandary as the canary in the cave, or urgent warning for the Church. This warning may reveal a painful symptom of the growing nihilism seeping into the blood stream of the Church. Dr. Brogdon concludes by offering a glimmering vision of hope and transformation, providing resources for both clergy and congregations for attending to perhaps one of the greatest issues confronting the Christian Church today.

>Johnny Bernard Hill, Ph.D.
>Associate Professor of Philosophy and Religion
>Claflin University, Orangeburg, South Carolina

1 Dying to Lead

Pastor Petros Roukas served as pastor of Tates Creek Presbyterian Church in Lexington, KY for five years, a church with a few hundred members. He was raised in Greece and was passionate about the Bible, his beliefs, and the people in his church, and he was loved by his congregation. Roukas had taught the Bible for years in churches in Muncie, Indiana and Bricktown, New Jersey baptized many into the faith, encouraged young people to attend seminary to become ministers and served the Tates Creek community for years. On September 22, Pastor Roukas left his home and did not return. He left suicide notes that were found by his wife Jan. He was struggling with depression for years and was under the care of a doctor. On September 29, the police found his body in a parked car at the Red River Gorge. He died by a gunshot wound to the head. His death devastated both the small, close-knit community and the church he faithfully served for a little more than five years.

Dr. Bryan Chapell, president of Covenant Theological Seminary, was invited to deliver the eulogy for his friend Petros. They had entered seminary together and been friends since that time. They had preached in each other churches, travelled together and shared many laughs. The text Chapell preached at his friend's funeral was Matthew 5:1-3 that ends with the encouragement, "Blessed are the poor in spirit for theirs is the kingdom of heaven." The idea of one who is poor in spirit was an apropos image of a kind soul who was troubled in the last years of his life. In the unenviable job of eulogizing his longtime friend, Chapell wrestled with the difficulties of his friend's untimely and tragic death. He confessed,

> I do not know why Petros could not pull out of the crash dive that spiraled him downward in recent months. I do not know why he was not able to cling to the Gospel truths that he ably preached for so long. But I do know that Jesus says that though we may lose our grip on him, he never loses his grip on us. In our fallen world, these corruptible bodies and minds

can go awry in ways that cause us temporarily to lose our grip on the better part of ourselves, and in those moments we do terrible things, but never do these things of earth pry God's children from the hand or heart of their heavenly Father.[1]

Dr. Chapell did his best to give meaning to the meaninglessness a family and church experiences when a husband or wife, father or mother and friend, who is also a pastor, commits suicide. As difficult as it is to imagine, this is the painful reality before the church today. This is the new chapter of ministry being written in large and small communities across this country. Pastors can go from years of effective ministry to a terrible death in a matter of months. Pastors are dying to lead. Moreover, their families and churches are left to deal with controversy, questions, and unbearable grief. In the same way Dr. Chapell and many other pastors do their best to give meaning to the meaninglessness of clergy suicide, I will attempt to give

---

[1] Bryan Chapell, "Funeral Message for Pastor Petros Roukas," in *The Hardest Sermons You'll Ever Have to Preach*. Kindle Version Bryan Chapell, ed. (Grand Rapids: Zondervan, 2011), 3641.

meaning to a problem whose breadth and depth was far greater than I was aware of a year ago.

Pastors: From Promising Beginnings to Troubled Ends

It is important to understand the kind of people who become pastors and serve as pastors because I've been around these people for the better part of twenty-three years as a minister and my lifetime of being a preacher's kid, I have come to understand the kind of people who become pastors and serve as pastors. Indeed, I have spent the past eight years serving as a seminary administrator and faculty member and have interacted with hundreds of people who accepted a call to ministry and come to seminary to prepare for a lifetime of ministry. While there are some scoundrels and a few superstars in the ministry, that is not the norm. Most are good-hearted people who faithfully serve the churches to which God calls them.

Pastors are men and women of deep faith, compassion for others and people who are selfless to a fault. Men and women who become pastors really believe in God. Their faith is not just rooted in head knowledge of Bible stories and commandments. Many have personal experiences that serve as fuel to their faith. They feel called, invoked by God to give witness to the love and power of God. Most pastors are people with big hearts. Pastors are very compassionate and enter ministry because they want to make a difference in people's lives. That is a major reason they preach with such passion. In the core of their being, they believe that preaching makes a difference. I've seen pastors preach so hard that it completely drains them of energy and strength. They do this not for show but because they give their all trying to get the message across about God.

Pastors are also selfless – often too selfless. They work long hours for little pay, sometimes no pay. Many do not have health insurance or retirement benefits. Yet they tithe a portion of their paychecks, give offerings every time the plate is passed, and often slip a few dollars into the hands of a person in need to tie them over until payday. They do this, as their own families are struggling to make ends meet and often do not know how they are going to pay their own bills.

Pastors are one of the first people to arrive in church and one of the last to leave. After they preach, they are often found picking up trash, cleaning bathrooms or, on occasion, cutting the church lawn. If something needs to done, most pastors are more than willing to do it.

This kind of dedication that contributes to the growth some churches experience ironically brings more work, more expectations, and more pressure. They give of themselves until there is little to nothing left.

Pastors are also deeply flawed individuals. On their best days, they are thoroughly imperfect. How ministers deal with their imperfections is the other side of pastoral ministry. While many pastors are faithful for the duration of their ministries, some are not. Some do not find healthy ways to work through their imperfections and taint years of faithful ministry in a season of weakness. Some pastors lose their way and betray the sacred trust churches put in them.

Media outlets and church circles can attest to these cases of clergy misconduct that range from extra-marital affairs, misappropriation of church or ministry funds, and substance abuse to child sexual abuse. However, things have changed. There are signs of deep problems among clergy in America. Some pastors have somehow lost their way and themselves in ministry to the extent that they are now committing suicide in alarming numbers. They are dying to lead.

Most pastors who serve Protestant congregations serve churches with less than one hundred members. In fact, one study found that half of America's 400,000 churches run about 75 in weekly attendance at worship. Today's popular media caricature of the superstar megachurch pastors does a grave disservice to the scores of men and women who serve small to medium size churches with their best energies and intentions and this popular caricature misrepresents the realities and challenges most pastors face today.

Someone is bound to ask, "Why write this book?" They may even contend that the frequency of clergy suicide in not that high – that it really is a rarity. Yet, every clergy suicide is a signal of deeper problems in the church. They are not random occurrences, and the rate of suicide is increasing among clergy. In the last two years alone, the alarming increase in the rate of clergy suicide signals that we need to talk about the issue.

God comes to us in hard and broken places. He promised his disciples to be with us always (Matt. 28:20). God's promise to never leave us nor forsake us is still true

(Heb. 13:5). God not only calls people to serve him as leaders and spokespersons, he is present with us through the hard places where that may lead. God is with those who minister in his name for the long haul – when times are good and when they are not good.

Two examples in Scripture bear this out. In 1 Kings 19, Elijah was at very hard place in his ministry and life. Elijah had prophesied that a terrible famine would come on the land and it did. The famine was sent by God but the time had come for rain. In 1 Kings 18, Elijah decided to go meet King Ahab to deliver the news and in doing so, proposed a dual between himself and four hundred and fifty prophets of Baal. In his mind, this would settle the question of who God was for the children of Israel. Elijah inquired of those who had gathered, "How long halt ye between two opinions? If the Lord be God, follow him: but if Baal, then follow him" (1 Kgs. 18:21, KJV). Elijah believed that this victory would represent a turning point, a change. Yet, when Jezebel received the news and vowed to kill him by the end of the day, Elijah fled. He ended up in a cave, sitting under a broom tree, complaining to God that he wanted to die. God came to Elijah in this lonely and dark place, God, the one who called him to be a prophet, came to him. He sent an angel to feed him and let him rest.

In John 21, Jesus came to Peter after he denied him, and now was despondent and dejected because he has failed his leader. Just before Jesus was arrested, Peter had told him that he was ready to go with him to prison or death. Peter was confident he would not forsake his Lord. That same night, however, he did just that. He betrayed Jesus, denying him three times.

The painful part of the denial was that after the third denial Jesus turned and looked Peter right in the eyes. Standing there before Jesus, he remembered the Savior's words and Peter was devastated and ashamed, embarrassed to face his friend.

Yet a few days after that dark night, Jesus prepared his friend some fish and talked with him about the love and feeding of His lambs. When Peter thought his days as a disciple were over, Jesus came to him with the gift of forgiveness and the offer of restoration. These stories teach a powerful truth. God does not abandon those he calls. He is with us, even in hard and broken places.

As hard as it is to think about, that same God was present in every hotel room, living room, vehicle, stairway, jail cell, and patio where a minister died by suicide. God was there. God saw it and felt their pain. God was present in their brokenness when some of them turned on their spouses and children in violence. God was present when their families and churches received the devastating news. All of this grieves the heart of God who wants us to do something substantive about the circumstances leading to this problem so that it does not keep happening.

We have to begin to wrap our minds around this issue. This discussion is a first step in making the Christian community aware of the problem of clergy depression and suicide. What does clergy suicide mean for today's church? We cannot sit and do nothing until another pastor commits suicide and then get shocked again. We must open our eyes to the painful realities of the dysfunctional ways we have done ministry for the past few decades and the fallout of frail men and women attempting to do hyper-ministry for so many years.

As you read perhaps a discussion will begin that will increase our capacity to empathize with families and congregations wrestling with the silent pain, deep wounds, and dysfunction that gives rise to these suicides. Perhaps, we will be pricked to commit to becoming advocates for clergy families and healthier congregational practices. As the dialogue grows, hopefully others will have more to say on these issues and will help us all imagine better ways to respond faithfully to God's call to ministry. The issues surrounding clergy suicide are complex. My hope is that the dialogue that is generated leads to systemic change.

2 Pastors and the Growing Problem of Suicide

In August 2014, the former presiding bishop of the International Communion of Charismatic Churches and pastor of Cedartown Christian Center, Bishop David Huskins, committed suicide. Bishop Huskins consecrated my former pastor and good friend, Fred Brown, to the bishopric and was a regular guest at every Holy Convocation and Family Conference Brown hosted in his Bluefield West Virginia congregation. I knew Huskins through my association with Bishop Fred Brown's network of pastors and ministers. The previous May, he preached in the Convocation and was as dynamic and impactful as ever. His message, from the Book of Acts, concluded with him speaking from his heart and ministering to the people. That night, he mentioned the trend of pastors committing suicide as a problem in the body of Christ.

I sat at a table with him and Bishop Brown after church that night and fellowshipped over pizza and salad. It was a great conference and everything seemed to be going well with him. Months later, the news that he died by suicide was hard to believe and, personally, hit me hard. I never imagined Bishop Huskins would die in that way. His death was another reminder of the growing problem of clergy suicide.

The Rash of Recent Clergy Suicides

For the past two years, an increasing number of pastors have resorted to suicide. In November 2013, Rev. Teddy Parker, the former pastor of Bibb Mount Zion Baptist Church in Macon, Georgia, committed suicide. A deacon within Parker's church told those at the funeral that the man dubbed "Macon's pastor" was a caring man. Two months earlier, Parker talked another man out of committing suicide and took time to call him every morning for the next three weeks to see how he was doing.[2] Parker, however, was

---

[2] See "Pastor Teddy Parker Commits Suicide as Congregation Waits for Him after Confessing Sometimes He "Can't Feel God," *Christian Today* (November 13 2013). Accessed on October 16, 2014; and Leonardo Blair, "Pastor Who Committed Suicide Sunday Stopped Man from Taking Own Life Weeks

hiding the fact that he was depressed and taking medication for that condition. His family was aware of the situation, but he kept this away from the church even while there were signs of a spiritual struggle he had with God and his faith. He had confessed in a sermon that sometimes he felt that God did not hear his prayers and this struggle led to a breaking point. On Sunday morning, November 10, he sent his wife and children to church ahead of him, with the understanding that he would follow later. Then he sat in his car outside his home and shot himself. When he didn't arrive at church as expected, his wife went looking for him and found him in his car. His death sent shockwaves across the country, and sadly drew attention to what was already a growing problem.

A month later, three other pastors committed suicide. Pastor Ed Montgomery was the former pastor of Full Gospel Christian Assemblies International Church in Hazel Crest, IL. He was grieving his wife who died. He reportedly shot himself in front of his mother and pleading son, expressing

---

Earlier…" *The Christian Post* (November 16, 2013). Accessed on October 16, 2014.

to them that he was hearing his dead spouse's voice and footsteps.

Pastor Isaac Hunter, founder of Orlando's Summit Church, took his life. He was the son of Joel Hunter, a prominent mega-church pastor and spiritual advisor to President Obama. The 36-year-old father of three had been in a downward spiral after first admitting to carrying on an affair with a staff member in 2012 and resigning.

Pastor Stephen Hightower killed himself on December 1, 2013. He was the founding pastor of ONEchurch in Athens and served in various positions in Georgia. He was a graduate of Regent University, completing both a Master of Divinity degree and a Doctorate of Strategic Leadership. Hightower wanted to establish a church for people considered outcasts and wrote about his passion for ministry on blogs for the School of Divinity. His zeal and zest for ministry died out under a mountain of student loan debt and a struggling church plant.

This past spring, Robert McKeehan was found hanging inside his home. He served as pastor of the Community Bible Church in High Point, North Carolina. McKeehan gave no signs of a man who was emotionally troubled. He started that day with a work out at his local gym and proceeded through the day with his usual activities even tweeting funny lines to several of his friends and making comments on Facebook. His death left members of his congregation and other supporters in shock.

A month later, 40-year-old George (DB) Antrim III committed suicide. He was a family pastor at Westwind Church in Johnston, Iowa. Just hours before Antrim's death, he had sat with his senior pastor to discuss the message the family pastor was expected to preach on Sunday, and gave no hint of any intention to harm himself. The father of two young sons was described as fun person who was always telling jokes.

Pastor Eddie Trull of Holly Springs Baptist Church in Franklin, North Carolina was found dead in a hotel room in Pigeon Forge, Tennessee from an apparent suicide. He was a pastor for twenty-five years of one of the most well populated churches in Franklin. One admirer described him as "a father of two, a husband of one, [and] a good man to all, [who] loved God…knew the Bible [and] killed himself." His death proved to be the beginning of difficult months on the horizon for the church.

There were more suicides over the summer. On June 23, Rev. Charles Moore, a seventy-nine year old retired Methodist pastor, stepped out of his car in a crowded shopping mall in Grand Seline, Texas and set himself on fire. Moore had been a lifelong advocate for social justice. Unlike many of the others who gave no explanation for why committed suicide, Moore left behind a trail of notes and a lifetime of activism to offer an explanation for his dramatic act. He expressed distress over his hometown, his alma mater, Southern Methodist University, and the United Methodist's church failure to deal with what he saw as social injustice on several fronts.[3]

Michael Mullis, former pastor of Near Calvary Baptist Church in Concord, North Carolina shot himself to death as deputies attempted to arrest him on child sex charges just days after authorities issued warrants for his arrest. Mullis had served as pastor of his congregation for 20 years, but resigned three years before taking his own life once he had come under investigation.

---

[3] Antonia Bloom, Rev. Charles Moore, Pastor Who Self-Immolated, Spent A Lifetime Protesting Injustice" *Huffington Post*, August 15, 2015.

Pastor Bill Scott served as an interim pastor of Charity Baptist Church in Lumbertown, North Carolina. In an unexplained fit of rage, he shot his wife and then killed himself in August 2014. The 68-year-old pastor and his 65-year-old wife were found on the patio of their home by their 16-year-old granddaughter. Scott was described as a well-educated man, who was down to earth with a way of injecting humor into his sermons. His wife of five years was described as dedicated to the church. Both of their deaths defied explanation by members of the congregation.

The same month, Bishop Huskins, who had been struggling with health problems and had been trying to slow down and take care of his health, committed suicide. He sent an email to the church about a month before his death. It read:

> It has been almost 20 years ago since I had open-heart surgery to repair a hole in my heart that had become critical. That started a series of mostly ignored warnings to take care of my heart health. Then in November, I had a mild heart attack (if there is such a thing) and that put me on a path to great

introspection of all the areas of my life I had not properly dealt with.

While I am grateful for all the Lord has allowed me to do, I knew sometimes I had let ministry be a substitute for God. I felt Him dealing with me to let go of areas and delegate and release and spend more time with Him and with people not just always in a pulpit. I had started that process much earlier with seeking to place others in charge of the church and daily duties but still had not relinquished the active roles.

Then over the past few weeks, I experienced congestive heart failure twice, which forced the cancellation of our annual conference, and now I have been told medically I am at the point of complete exhaustion while still dealing with chronic congestive heart failure. After three nights in ICU and another two-night regular hospital stay along with several follow-up heart procedures and this past week a Transient Ischemic Attack (minor stroke) and the adaptations of all the medicines ... and the on-going recovery process and having been admitted to bed rest, I am now forced to make some significant and important changes immediately.

Even though I have been feeling it and talking about it for a couple of years. The next 90 days minimal will be intensive times of physical therapy and monitoring both heart and neck arteries and avoiding the threat of another heart attack or stroke... I am submitting to the precaution. As most of you know, I wrote over a year ago about the need for many of us to take a break, get counsel, seek a sabbatical, or otherwise make changes. We even held a January conference around that concept. I put a plan in place for a sabbatical or even a succession plan. We discussed many of these subjects, but I then returned quickly to the rigors of ministry. Now it is medically required and physically necessary for me to adapt.

... The truth is, however, the need for a real sabbatical is long overdue. The effects of this mini-stroke and the medicines along with the energy lost from the congestive heart failure keep me very confused, often times unable to articulate my thoughts clearly and then, also, all the physical limits and battles. I am thankful that they say all that is temporary and will be over in time.[4]

Yet, the heavy demand ministry placed on Huskins as presiding bishop of a large network of churches, pastor of two congregations, sought out international speaker, host of a weekly radio show, and guest on Trinity Broadcasting Network (TBN) proved to be too much. The effect on his health was complicated by the medication he had been prescribed. The pressures of his position and the struggles he was experiencing with his health were contributing factors in his tragic death.

Pastoral suicides are only the tip of the iceberg. There is evidence that pastor's wives and children are increasingly turning to suicide. Last January, Harriet Deison, wife of the pastor of Park Cities Presbyterian Church, shot herself to death while sitting in her car. She did not leave a suicide note but instead, in what appeared to be a spontaneous

---

[4] Mark Andrews, "Charismatic Church Network Leads Dies in Apparent Suicide," *CharismaNews.com* (August 27, 2014). Accessed on August 28, 2014.

action, purchased a gun at a local gun shop, then killed herself moments later.

Popular mega church pastor, Rick Warren lost his 27-year-old son, Matthew, to suicide after a lifelong battle with mental illness. He had struggled from birth with depression and suicidal thoughts. After what his father described as a "fun evening" as a family, young Warren took his life "in a momentary wave of despair at his home."[5]

In 2009, prominent Southern Baptist leader, Frank Page, lost his at 32-year-old daughter, Melissa Page Strange, to suicide. Melissa had endured myriad challenges, from Hodgkin's lymphoma — a form of cancer —to prescription drug addiction.

Research for this book discovered twenty-three suicides involving pastors, a Catholic priest, and youth ministers as well as members of their families. Yet, these cases are only a sample that such a cursory search can yield. Those in pastoral and denominational leadership know that many unreported cases never hit the media, and many of which we are unaware. Between 2006 and 2013, for example

---

[5] "Pastor Rick Warren's Son Matthew Commits Suicide After Lifelong Battle With Mental Illness" ABCNews Online

the South Carolina state convention of Southern Baptists, alone, reported seven other cases.

Too many congregations have gone through the trauma and grief associated with the pastoral suicide. Most of us who have been in the church for any length of time, never imagined a day when, pastors would be committing suicide at such a high rate. Christian leaders across the country express shock over this growing trend and are trying to understand why so many pastors turn to suicide to end the suffering and pain experienced in their lives or ministries.

This rash of suicides is not new! The opening years of the twenty-first century were great for many Baptist and nondenominational churches. Congregations were growing and pastors were busy preaching, teaching, counseling, networking, and leading their churches. Along with 8 a.m. and 11 a.m. services, there were afternoon services, revivals, conferences, business meetings, church meetings, visitations, funerals, and church squabbles to address every other week. In some cases, what we thought of as successful, cutting-edge ministry was slowly killing the men and women of God.

In many cases, there were warning signs of the developing trend. As early 2009, there was a rash of clergy suicides, but no one flagged it as a major concern. That year, in North Carolina, David Treadway, who was 42, committed suicide. His wife found the pastor of the fast growing Sandy Ridge Baptist Church in Hickory, dead in his car Sunday morning as she was leaving for church. Within the next four years, two more clergy in North Carolina and three in South Carolina killed themselves.

Were we just not paying attention? Were we too busy attending church conferences? Were we trying to protect the façade of successful ministry? Could the recent flurry of suicides been averted? We can never know this but it is worth asking.

Rush to Judgment and Criticism

The overwhelming number of clergy suicides has finally called us to attention now, and there is much discussion across the country about the issue. Such discussion helps to bring the problem to the forefront where we can address it. Yet if we focus on individual clergy moral failures without giving due attention to the systemic factors affecting churches today, we will miss the opportunity to bring healing and wholeness to those who have given so much.

We must all be deeply concerned, however, about the cold judgmentalism of critics who see these pastors as failures because they committed suicide. Many are quick to condemn these men and women to an eternity in hell.

Pastoral suicide traumatizes congregations and forces family members to grieve publically before the world as news outlets pour into town to report the story. Who helps them process the grief they experienced and who cares about these congregations in the aftermath? The tendency to trivialize and minimize the pressures of ministry remains in place and the difficult task of pastoring a contemporary congregation does not receive the attention it deserves. How do we collectively address such a complex problem with the shallow thinking dominating social and online news media? This tendency to trivialize the problems contemporary clergy face hinders our ability to adequately address the phenomenon of clergy suicide.

A second concern is the tendency to focus on individual moral failures of clergy without giving adequate attention to the systemic factors affecting contemporary churches. In the world of bloggers and social media, the widespread view among those who love to track clergy misconduct is that some commit suicide to hide sins that are about to be exposed. In the Mullins' case for example, he was about to be arrested. Yet, his suicide is only one among many that had nothing to do with misconduct.

These critics believe that many pastors lead double lives and instead of facing the truth and consequences of their actions, opt to kill themselves. Granted, the number of clergy suicides that involve some form of misconduct is too high and lends itself to the insinuation that the two phenomena are linked. Yet, not all clergy who commit suicide are involved in misconduct. Therefore, another question of what is driving alarming levels of misconduct arises where a contributing factor is the threat of facing the consequences of misconduct. It is certainly more complex than just assigning blame to these circumstances.

This line of thinking fails to recognize the personal, familial, and congregational issues driving pastors and church leaders to destructive habits in the first place. We need a systemic approach that determines the driving force behind both the misconduct and suicide. It is quite possible that burnout, disillusionment, and apathy are some of the reasons for the prevalence of both.

There are individual and congregational or ministerial factors at work in clergy misconduct. Mullins may have committed suicide because he wanted an easy way out, but some pastors have been disillusioned with ministry and are so deeply involved in dysfunctional behavior for so many years that suicide seems the only option to them. It may be that death seems to promise rest and a cessation from toil that ministry cannot give them.

The death of Zachery Tims, popular pastor of New Destiny Christian Center in Apopka, Florida, points to such a suggestion. Tims had been struggling with drug addiction for years, and died of overdose in a New York hotel. Possibly, his drug use was a mask for deeper disappointments with ministry and an inability to experience the victorious life he often preached about to other for years.

In reality, clergy problems are a part of larger issues affecting the American congregational system. The American church is in crisis: attendance is steadily declining and increasing numbers of ministers are disillusioned with what they experience in their work. According to one study, "On any given Sunday, the vast majority of Americans are absent from church…and as the American population continues to grow, the church falls further and further behind. If trends continue, by 2050 the percentage of Americans attending church will be half the 1990 figure."[6] For a host of reasons, Americans are not attending church and it is gaining more attention, decreasing ministerial job satisfaction, and increasing the stress and disillusionment in ministry.

Julia Duin addressed this trend in, *Quitting Church: Why the Faithful Are Fleeing*. Duin found that more Americans are leaving, or not attending, church, are turned off by the church, and have little interest in being involved with what goes on in churches. One reason is the infighting and political games within the church. Her work raises deeper questions about why church has lost appeal for so many. Thousands of Americans annually quit church because they are turned by far too many toxic and

---

[6] David T. Olson, *The American Church in Crisis* (Grand Rapids: Zondervan, 2008), 16.

dysfunctional congregations. This has only worsened since G. Lloyd Rediger's controversial 1997 work, *Clergy Killers: Guidance for Pastors and Congregations under Attack,* was written. Rediger drew attention to toxic cultures in some congregations and exposed a troubling dynamic in these churches. Some individuals or groups are bent on bringing harm to the pastor and their families. These individuals and groups cause as much trouble as they possibly can within a congregation.[7] After this, he highlighted the devastating effect these actions have on clergy self-esteem, causing such symptoms as high rates of depression, increased stress, and serious health problems.

A third issue for American churches is nominalism. Not only are some congregations contentious, but many are not cultivating the spirituality they preach and sing about. For example, George Barna recently reported the following findings:

- Biweekly attendance at worship services is, by believer's own admission, generally the only time many worship God.

---

[7] G. Lloyd Rediger, *Clergy Killers* (Louisville: Westminster John Knox 1997).

- Eight out of every ten people do not feel they have entered into the presence of God, or experienced a connection with Him, during the worship service.

- Half of those surveyed did not feel that they have entered into the presence of God or experienced a genuine connection with God during the past year.

- Only one out of every four churched believers said that when they worship God, they expect Him to be the primary beneficiary of their worship. Most people say they expect to get the most from the experience.[8]

These examples are evidence of, what Barna termed, a revolution –a reference to the growing number of Christians who no longer attend congregational worship. That a growing numbers of Americans (even born again Christians) are leaving congregations, is a reflection of deep issues that need addressing. These are surely factors influencing clergy emotional health and vocational satisfaction.

---

[8] George Barna, Revolution (Carol Stream IL: BarnaBooks, 2005), 31-32.

The issue of clergy suicide, therefore, is far more pervasive and complex than most news articles suggest. It speaks to entrenched problems of brokenness and dysfunctional congregations, unrealistic clergy demands, lack of adequate preparation for the rigors of ministry, and insufficient support for clergy and their families. Broken congregational systems and models of ministry replicate the same outcome. To our collective dismay, that is exactly what we are seeing – more suicides.

We cannot rush to judgment nor place the blame on dysfunctional ministers. Instead, we must question what is really going on. We cannot blame a few bad preachers who do not know how to handle stress as we stand by doing nothing as we continue to see an increasing number of clergy – and clergy family members turn to suicide as the ultimate solution to their pain. We must look deeper.

Looking Deeper

The sign of hope is that some leaders are beginning to ask the right questions and address the issue systemically. There are signs that a national conversation is underway that recognizes the complexity of the matrix of issues we are facing. Some leaders are beginning to recognize the unique pressures pastor's face and the signs of unfathomable problems in the American congregational system.

Last year, Bishop T. D. Jakes commented on the recent flurry of suicides, that, "pastors are still far too overworked, underpaid and discouraged by the reactions of some of their congregation when something goes wrong." He discussed the fact that, along with preaching regularly, pastors must perform a wide variety of duties: perform weddings and funerals, keep track of members, organize charitable and fundraising events, counsel and pray with people, and keep members secrets. Further, he underscored the irony that in all this a pastor must "stand up and be examined by his congregation on Sunday."[9]

The unique and difficult pressures that pastors confront daily may contribute to what Brian Dodd saw as the situation in which "pastors have the third highest rates of suicide among professions behind only doctors and

---

[9] Nigel Boys, "T. D. Jakes Responds to Recent Pastor Suicides: Pastors Expected to do a lot and Expected to Survive on Crumbs," *AllChristianNews.Com*. (December 19, 2013). Accessed on September 18, 2014.

attorneys."[10] Such a statistic is worth further examination since many who prepare for ministry are not prepared for such difficult realities.

Jennifer LeClaire of *Charisma News* expressed serious concern for the growing trend of clergy suicide, insisting that we need to take a closer look at the issue. She cited statistics by the Schaeffer Institute regarding pastors and depression, burnout, health, low pay, spirituality, relationships and longevity, and concluded with starling statistics about clergy.[11] The study found that 70% constantly fight depression, 71% experience burned out, and 72% say they only study the Bible when they are preparing for sermons. 80% believe pastoral ministry has negatively affected their families and 70% say they do not have a close friend. It also reports that 80% of seminary and Bible school graduates will leave the ministry within five years of graduation.[12] The truth is men and women do not enter

---

[10] Brian Dodd, "Pastors and Suicide," *Brian Dodd on Leadership* (April 10, 2013). Accessed on September 24, 2014.

[11] Jennifer LeClaire, "Why are so many Pastors Committing Suicide?" *CharismaNews* (December 11, 2013). Accessed on September 18 2014.

[12] Richard J. Krejcir, "Statistics on Pastors: What is Going on with the Pastors in America," *The Schaeffer Institute* (2007). Accessed on September 19, 2014.

seminary and spend thousands of dollars on an education so they can spend years of their lives in toxic and dysfunctional congregations. Most ministers do not expect ministry to be this difficult.

This kind of data is helpful in beginning to assess the larger context of contemporary pastoral ministry. Further, it may help us understand why pastors are leaving the ministry in high numbers. They are working under an incredible amount of stress and pressure. Now a small number are committing suicide. The same factors driving some clergy to leave the ministry, drives some to commit suicide and show other signs of serious dysfunction.

Church leaders are beginning to consider the issue of clergy mental health exhibited in this dysfunction. An emerging theme in the narratives regarding clergy suicide is untreated depression and there is there is a real problem with depression among clergy. Many pastors struggle with depression, yet for a variety of reasons including fear of appearing unspiritual, fear of losing their pastorate, need to protect their families from scrutiny, or lack of a non-judgmental support system, choose to not disclose their struggle or seek treatment while their condition only worsens.

Reportedly, Parker, whose wife found him in the driveway of their home with a self-inflicted gunshot wound, struggled with manic-depressive disorder, yet, hid it from his church. His death has awakened awareness about depression among clergy and mental health professionals began writing articles about depression and other related issues.

In one essay on depression in ministry, Paul David Tripp discussed four potential setups for what he calls the discouragement-depression cycle: unrealistic expectations, family tensions, fear of man instead of fear of God, and kingdom confusion – or glory seeking.[13] Though Tripp only scratches the surface, his analysis is helpful at pointing to some factors contributing to clergy suicide.

A discussion of depression in ministry requires us to think systemically about two things. First, depression and suicide do not only affect clergy but millions of Americans.

---

[13] Paul David Trip, "Dealing with Depression in Ministry" *ChurchLeaders.com* (Date unknown). Accessed on September 18 2014.

Second, we need not have a simplistic and monolithic conversation about such a complex issue.

Stress, depression, and suicide have reached alarming levels in every segment of our society. The Center for Disease and Control (CDC) reported that antidepressant drug use in the U. S. has increased fourfold from 2.4 percent between 1988-1994 to 10.8 percent between 2007-2010, making them one of the most frequently used classes of medications by Americans aged 18-44.[14] We must view these finding in light of the fact that suicide is one of the leading causes of death for Americans, and depression is one of the major causes of suicide. Pastors are a part of a larger national crisis; thousands of Americans suffer from chronic stress and depression; many of them turn to suicide.

We must also examine how we handle mental health issues in the church and broader Christian community. Generally, issues of both mental health and suicide are taboo among those who are often not adequately educated about mental health issues. Such lack makes it difficult to

---

[14] "Health, United States, 2013 includes special section on prescription drugs," *The Center for Disease and Control* (May 14, 2014). Accessed on September 19, 2014.

encourage and provide opportunities for leaders who have mental health concerns to be cared for. Moreover, churches often hold biblical and theological beliefs that make it difficult for pastors and congregants to be educated on mental health issues or to seek out mental health professionals when needed.

Parishioners often hold their pastors to an unrealistic standard. They feel that because God called a man or woman to ministry and is with them, parishioners expect pastors to be spiritual people who are capable of handling the stresses of life and ministry without outside assistance. Such attitudes discourage pastors who may need it, from reaching out for help from a therapist or other mental health specialist. Such action would be seen as a sign of weak faith and a deficient spirituality.

The conversation about this issue has already begun. Clergy today face many challenges and without having the necessary and adequate support structures structures in place to handle them. Some are mired in misconduct of various kinds, while others are battling severe, chronic depression or other mental illnesses. For these and other reasons, some are turning to suicide. In the next chapter, I will provide closer analysis of the issue of why, for some troubled pastors, suicide seems to be their only alternative.

3 Helping Troubled Pastors

Ministry is doing something to pastors today that we did not see during the final two decades of the twentieth century. We need to assess what is going on and we need to do this in a comprehensive manner. Since this situation has been percolating in the church for years, we can't solve this problem overnight. Yet, with God's aid, we can mount an effort to help clergy who are in trouble so that no man or woman of God feels that suicide is their only option.

Hopefully, what I am relating will encourage the faith community to take the necessary steps to address this sobering matter in a serious manner. We have to start somewhere, and a first step in this larger endeavor is to understand where we are. From the data unearthed on clergy suicide, we can make some preliminary observations.

Representative Cases of Clergy Suicide

Name	Race/Gender	Date of Suicide	Church Name/Denomination	Cause of Death	Circumstances Surrounding Death
W. Phillip West	White male	November 14, 2014	Pastor Harbor View Church James Island, SC Presbyterian USA	Unknown	Unknown.
Mickey Shealy	White male	October 30 2014	Pastor Christ Church Dalton, GA Presbyterian EPC	Unknown	Unknown
David Huskins	white male	August 25 2014	Pastor Cedartown Christian Center Atlanta Nondenominational	Gunshot wound	Declining health (heart), complications with medication
Bill Scott	white male	August 2014	Interim pastor Charity Baptist Church Lumberton, NC	Gunshot wound	Shot his wife and himself. Cause of dispute unknown
Charles Moore	white male	June 23 2014	Retired pastor United Methodist Church Grand Saline ,TX	Self-immolation	Haunted by past lynchings, wanted death to inspire social reform
Michael Mullins	white male	July 2014	Former pastor Near Calvary Baptist Church Concord, NC	Gunshot wound	Deputies were attempting to arrest him on child sex charges
George DB Antrim	white male	May 1 2014	Pastor Westwind Church Johnston IA Nondenominational Evangelical	Unknown	Unknown

Name	Race/Sex	Date	Role/Church	Cause	Notes
Scott Sechrist	white male	May 2014	Pastor First Baptist Church Morrisville PA	Gunshot wound	Under investigation for molestation of 9 year old girl in 1992. One week before trial.
Nicholas Henshaw	white male	May 2014	Youth Pastor Capo Beach Calvary Church Ft. Collins CO Nondenominational	Suffocation by way of asphyxiation with helium	Arrested and charged with sexual assault of child. Out on bond
Father Vladimir Dziadek	white male	May 2014	Priest St. Josephs Parish Tampa FL Roman Catholic	Hanging	Depression. Under investigation for embezzlement of funds. Death occurred in parish
Robert McKeehan	white male	April 2014	Pastor Community Bible Church High Point NC Nondenominational	Hanging	Unknown
Matthew Warren	white male	April 2013	Pastor's son Saddleback Community Church Mission Viejo CA Baptist	Gunshot	Depression
Eddie Trull	white male	April 2013	Pastor Holly Springs Baptist Church Macon County NC	Unknown	Unknown
Teddy Parker	black male	November 2013	Pastor Bibb Mt Zion Baptist Church Macon GA	Gunshot	Depression
Stephen J. Hightower	white male	December 1 2013	Pastor ONEchurch Athens GA Evangelical Presbyterian Church	Gunshot	Despondent over heavy student loan debt from seminary and a failed church plant

Name	Race/Sex	Date	Role/Church	Method	Circumstances
Ed Montgomery	black male	December 10 2013	Pastor Full Gospel Christian Assemblies International Church Hazel Crest IL Nondenominational	Gunshot	Grieving loss of wife
Harriet Deison	white female	January 2013	Spouse Park Cities Presbyterian Church Dallas TX	Gunshot	Depression
Isaac Hunter	white male	December 2013	Pastor Summit Church Orlando, FL Nondenominational	Gunshot	Had an affair, resigned from church
Terry Greer	white male	January 2013	Pastor Mt Vernon United Methodist Gardendale AL	Attempted suicide stopped by police	Shot his wife and daughter.
H. Randy Stevens	black male	September 2010	Pastor Undisclosed Church Columbus GA Baptist	Unknown	Exposed by gay lover of 15 years. Killed himself at church
Matthew Jarrell	white male	May 25 2011	Pastor Open Door Baptist Church Mesquite TX	Unknown	In jail facing charges of sexual assault
Nicholas William Minerva	white male	June 2011	Pastor Trinity Baptist Fellowship in South Phoenix Nondenominational	Unknown	Served a warrant investigating internet conversations with a 14 year old girl
Zachery Tims	black male	August 14, 2011	Pastor New Destiny Christian Center Orlando, FL Nondenominational	Overdosed on cocaine-heroin mixture	Divorced because of affairs and drug use, battle with drugs

David Treadway	white male	September 2009	Pastor Sandy Ridge Baptist Church Hickory NC	Committed suicide in parked car	Unknown
Brent Hogan	white male	November 2006	Pastor Community Presbyterian Church Pittsburgh, PA Presbyterian USA	Found dead in a motel room. Overdose of alcohol and aspirin	Pending TV probe by KDKA-TV of a minister involved in sexual relationship with a man. Died night before story was to air.
Petros Roukas	white male	September 29 2004?	Pastor Tates Creek Presbyterian Church Lexington KY Presbyterian Church of America	Committed suicide in car by gunshot	Depression
Seven unnamed Southern Baptist Ministers[15]		2012	Pastors South Carolina Southern Baptist	Unknown	Unknown

[15] Rudy Gray, "Suicide: A Tragic Mistake," *Baptistcourier.com* (December 6 2012). Accessed on September 24, 2014.

45

Observations

1. The majority of the pastors are Baptist, Nondenominational, or Presbyterian.

2. Eleven of the twenty-one suicides among pastors involved clergy misconduct of some kind.

3. Most pastors are in the South – the region that we refer to as the Bible Belt. Within this region, several states have had at least two incidents of clergy suicide in a relatively short period: North Carolina, South Carolina, Georgia, and Florida. According to one online article, South Carolina has had seven pastors to commit suicide, which is more than any state in the south.

4. All pastors are male. There are no reported cases of clergy suicide among female pastors.

5. Four African American pastors have committed suicide in the past five years: two were nondenominational and two were Baptist.

6. The mode of suicide ranged across a broad spectrum: twelve by gunshot, two by hanging, one by suffocation, one died by self-immolation, two by drug overdose, and nine unknown. Four pastors were found dead in a hotel, three in different towns than place of residency. Three pastors died on church grounds. Five died at home. One died in jail. Five died in their car.

What could some of these things mean? First, it is alarming that many of the pastors are Baptist and nondenominational. This raises the possibility that Baptist and nondenominational pastors in the South are not getting the support they need when they struggle with mental illness or when they are in trouble personally. These pastors are left to struggle alone. These churches have a congregational polity structure and there may be something endemic to this mode of governance and clergy suicide. These churches are autonomous. They are not connected to a district or to a jurisdiction of churches. They do not have a presiding bishop or ruling elders who oversee churches and pastors. Baptist and nondenominational churches are independent, often with solo pastors.

There is nothing inherently wrong with the traditional Baptist church structure. Baptist Congregations are free to join associations and conventions while they maintain their autonomy and govern themselves according to their own bylaws and constitution. However, one liability of this form of governance in the culture of today's church may be that pastors are left on their own without built in denominational support and feel isolated. The feeling of isolation can easily go undetected for a while. One must notice the high numbers of Baptist and nondenominational pastors doing ministry on their own.

Second, it is noteworthy that most of the pastors who committed suicide serve churches in the Bible Belt – the region in the south-eastern and south-central part of the country in which socially conservative evangelical Protestantism is a significant part of the culture. It is characterized by being home to a large number of people who engage in high levels of religious activity, hold a literal interpretation of the Bible, as well as conservative theological beliefs and actively encourage others to believe in Jesus. Anecdotally, Christians in these states exhibit high rates of church attendance, activity, and religious zeal.

Whether these levels are actually higher than other parts of the United States is debatable, the sub-culture may be seen as a factor in the higher proportion of clergy who commit suicide. Churches in the region have rigid ethical standards. They place stringent moral demands on members and especially pastors, giving them little to no room for error. Pastors are expected to perform at the highest level under pressure of the threat of losing one's job.

The pressure is compounded when they hear of other pastors being dismissed from churches for a variety of reasons. For example, an article written by Rudy Gray in the *Baptist Courier* found that South Carolina Baptist Churches have the highest rate of pastoral terminations of surrounding states.[16] The specter of termination puts pastors under an incredible amount of pressure. Pastors in the Bible Belt know that a mistake can have devastating consequences on their tenure. Worse yet, if the church perceives the pastor

---

[16] Rudy Gray, "Pastoral Termination: An Epidemic?" *Baptistcourier.com* (January 3, 2013). Accessed on September 24, 2014.

can't get the job done (sometimes as determined by arbitrary standards), the result can be a vote to terminate.

This creates difficulties for clergy with mental health or personal problems. They are forced to keep quiet in order to keep the church from losing confidence in their ability to lead the church. The fear of losing one's job pushes pastors deeper into mental illness and dysfunction because they honestly have no place to turn. Beyond the structural limitations with independently governed churches, there are theological ones too. The traditional theology of Baptists and the overly spiritual theology of some nondenominational churches do not give room for issues like mental illness.

Many Baptists believe in the power of prayer. There is an expectation that earnest prayer offered to God in faith will yield results. God can fix it. Nondenominational churches face similar theological challenges. In some nondenominational churches, particularly those who believe in the gifts of the Spirit and miracles, there is little room for pastors with mental illness. God is a healer. God works miracles where there is faith. Thus pastors in these churches are put in a predicament when they preach and lead about a God who heals and works miracles while they are depressed and struggling with personal demons. This requires a different kind of theology and it is incredibly difficult to get churches to amend theologies that they have grown accustomed to, even if they do not give meaning to unique challenges they face in life. The easy thing to do is question the pastor's faith and blame them for their flaws.

Third, there is no denying the correlation between misconduct and suicide. Most clergy suicides involve misconduct. This suggests there are too many pastors engaged in misconduct, some of which is illegal. Misconduct is a real problem and it appears that things are not improving but instead worsening. What is very disturbing about this misconduct is that women and children are victims of violent and exploitative acts from male clergy. It is clear that churches are not always safe places for them and there is much work to do in this area. It is quite possible that there is a correlation between abuse of women and children and the patriarchal theology in these traditions.

As I mentioned earlier, the problem of misconduct is systemic. It is a manifestation of dysfunction at multiple levels of denominational and congregational systems. These systems produce clergy who are exposed to both dysfunction and abuse years before they become participants in it themselves. This exposure does exonerate these men and women, but forces us to address the larger systems at work. Unless we do, misconduct will continue to undermine the public's trust in churches.

    The growth in the numbers of clergy involved in misconduct increases the likelihood for more suicides. Clergy such as Nicholas Henshaw and Scott Sechrist were facing criminal charges related to their misconduct. They turned to suicide to escape facing the humiliation of going from an ordained minister to being a convicted criminal. Others were under investigation for theft of church funds. In one incident, there was an extra-marital affair. They all turned to suicide as an easier escape than the long road to accountability and healing. But fear of exposure is only part of the increasing reason of clergy suicides. There is often fear on a deeper level- the inner fear that there is no hope or meaning in life and ministry. This hopelessness drives some to suicide. More than fear, some have lost the ability to care anymore: they have ceased to care about themselves, they have ceased to care about the church, and they have ceased to care about life.

Nihilism among Clergy

*Elijah was afraid and fled for his life. He went to Beersheba, a town in Judah, and he left his servant there. Then he went on alone into the wilderness, traveling all day. He sat down under a solitary broom tree and prayed that he might die. "I have had enough, L*ORD*," he said. "Take my life, for I am no better than my ancestors who have already died.* (1 Kgs. 19:1-4, NLT)

Forty days after sitting under the broom tree in the wilderness and telling God to take his life, Elijah ended up in a cave. God comes to him there and confronts him with a good question, "What are you doing here?" After the great victory at Mt. Carmel, the corrupt king Ahab and his idolatrous wife, Jezebel, were still in charge. And Israel was still unfaithful. It looked as if the prophet had wasted his time, energy, and life on a futile endeavor. His zeal for the Lord was gone, and he felt that had been left alone, abandoned by everyone – even the God for whom he spoke. Elijah's response to God was that, "… I, even I only, am left, and they seek to take [my life] away" (1 Kings 19:10).

Elijah was despondent. It looked like nothing had changed and he thought that he was better off by himself, better off if he quit his prophetic work, and better off if he was dead! Elijah's story of having completely expended himself, seemingly for nothing, resonates with some contemporary pastors who have said to God, "I've had enough." What a place to find a prophet – in a cave!

One of the saddest aspects of the trend of clergy suicide is that many of those who have killed themselves were found alone! Whether in a hotel room, at home, or in a car, they die alone. How can this happen to men and women who know the teachings of the Bible as well as they do? How can this happen to pastors who have themselves proclaimed God's promise of comfort and support to so many others. How do they end up like this?

To some extent they have not only lost their way in navigating the challenges of ministry, they have lost hope in God and life has become meaningless. Hopelessness has been bubbling underneath sermons, hospital visits, Bible studies, counseling sessions, business meetings, and other pastoral duties for quite some time. According to a 2000 *New York Times* article,

Members of the clergy now suffer from obesity, hypertension and depression at rates higher than do most other Americans. In the last decade, their use of antidepressants has risen, while their life expectancy has fallen. Many would change jobs if they could. Public health experts who have led the studies say that there is no simple explanation of why so many members of a profession once associated with rosy-cheeked longevity have become unhealthy and unhappy.[17]

Paul Vitello linked the pervasive unhappiness and depression among clergy to their failure or refusal to take time off. Though this is partly true, it does not get at the root of the problem plaguing some clergy today. They are not just worn out and experiencing burnout. It is much deeper.

When pastors are taking their own lives in numbers like the ones we have seen in the past two years, they have become victim to the ever-growing and pervasive influence of nihilism. The word comes from the Latin term "nihil" meaning nothingness. As a philosophical concept, it implies

---

[17] Paul Vitello, "Taking a Break from the Lord's Work," *The NewYorkTimes.com* (August 1 2010). Accessed on October 17, 2014.

that the world or life lacks purpose or meaning. Two words, hopelessness and meaninglessness, best convey the meaning of nihilism. For what is life without hope and meaning? Is it worth living?

Friedrich Nietzsche wrote about nihilism in nineteenth century Europe, describing it as a failure of foundational beliefs and values to give meaning to the world.[18] When beliefs cannot give meaning to existential realities, beliefs are rejected. At its core, nihilism is the rejection of a set of beliefs that fail to give hope and meaning to lived realities. Pastors, who face the nihilism brought about by inadequate beliefs, are sent into a tailspin, becoming prime candidates for dysfunction and destructive behaviors such as suicide.

The fact these pastors know the Bible and have a theological vision of how things could be in the world and church are part of the problem of nihilism. A person wrestling with nihilism is a person with a certain disconnect between their experience of ministry in the church and the

---

[18] Lewis Brogdon, *Hope on the Brink: Understanding the Emergence of Nihilism in Black America* (Eugene: Cascade, 2013), 16.

beliefs that were instrumental in their choice to enter ministry. The disconnect is deep.

For some of these pastors, it is clear that the nice and tidy beliefs of yester years or the clean theology they learned in Bible school or seminary was of little use in today's culturally diverse, complex world. The theology and doctrine they were taught really does not help them make sense of the real-life situations they face in everyday ministry to real people. The formulas for success do not work quite as easily when they move from paper to real life. The failure of these formulas and surface answers to make sense of the deeper questions arising from ministry causes both dissonance and high levels of job dissatisfaction.

Regrettably, many do not even have a safe space to wrestle with these issues. Hence, pastors often bifurcate their emotions, putting on a façade that masks deep pain and questions. Sadly, some fall into the trap of living a lie to appease their congregations and to keep their jobs. They tell their churches "everything is alright" and that "things are getting better in the world," while they personally feel the opposite is true. There are smiles and sermons of assurance on the surface but have deep insecurities and questions troubling their spirit.

For many, the pulpit has become a hazardous place to raise deep questions or to challenge closely cherished beliefs. Evangelical parishioners expect pastors – even young pastors – to have their theology worked out, and they expect that theology to, wholeheartedly, reflect beliefs they have held to for years. In the end, one has to wrestle with these questions alone.

Some pastor's lack of theological training leaves them at a significant disadvantage in dealing with the moral, existential, and ideological complexities of ministry. Without knowledge of others within the Christian tradition who have raised similar issues, these pastor fail to realize that the questions with which they wrestle are not new. Because of this lack, they are often ill prepared to work through complex biblical, theological, and philosophical problems.

They are stuck in meaninglessness with pat answers, proof texts, and no one to talk with about ministry and life. Worse yet, they see the fruit of it in congregations with large numbers of nominal Christians and empty amens from people who have no interest in living out the radical nature of the gospel. Their churches are nothing more than social clubs and places to claim political power. Often in these cases, the pastor is caught in the middle and is not taken seriously as a God-called leader. This really gets old for people who believe faith and God are supposed to make a difference and has a crushing effect on one's hope.

      Like Elijah in the cave, these pastors, frequently, feel they have done little to make a difference in the world. They look around and it seems nothing has changed. In addition, far too many blame themselves for this sad state of affairs. In such meaningless conditions, some turn on themselves and towards reckless, irresponsible, and self-destructive behaviors. Some may even reason, "If this is all a game, then what does it matter if I abuse alcohol or drugs?" These feelings of meaninglessness and hopelessness breed conditions that land promising pastors in a hotel room alone with drugs or a gun and a tragic end. A nihilistic pastor would rather die than explore the possibility of a new chapter in ministry. They choose death for themselves and those who feel most trapped in the prison of meaninglessness may kill others. This is the stuff of nihilism, of nothingness.

Real Concern for Clergy Today

Consider what Elijah said to God. He said he had enough. In fact, Elijah went as far as to admit that he wanted to die. He was not only ready to give up on his calling; he was ready to give up on life itself. He parked himself under a broom tree and told God, "I've had enough." Then he laid down and went to sleep. Interestingly, God does not respond immediately. Instead, he sends an angel to Elijah and lets the prophet eat and get some rest. This goes on for forty days. Elijah journeys to a cave and then the Lord comes to him, again, with the question, "What are you doing here?" There are a lot of Elijah's in ministry today who have reached the point where they have had enough and they want to die. The difference between Elijah's story and the tragic story of these pastors is that Elijah wanted God to let him die. He did not take matters into his own hands.

This biblical story illustrates my belief that pastors do not just suddenly decide to commit suicide. Those that take this way out have, usually, mulled and wrestled over the decision for some time. Perhaps, many have told God how they were feeling about ministry and life. They may have even told God what they wanted to do, and, like Elijah, they slept on the idea. All this they did alone – in isolation. No one knew that while they were preparing and preaching sermons, teaching Bible study, shaking hands and hugging members, they were also often sitting alone thinking about ending their ministries and lives.

Yet, they also probably wondered how things had gotten to that point, and there was some disappointment regarding both themselves and their ministry. They must have resented the fact that they had been there for so many while no one was there for them. My heart aches for them and a church culture that has come to this. Nevertheless, if they were thinking about suicide for days, weeks and months before taking action, there are others thinking about such a decision right now.

Before another pastor takes his or her life, we must open our eyes to some serious concerns regarding what this trend means for the larger, contemporary church culture. Statistics do not lie regarding the severity of clergy stress that may contribute to suicide:

- 13% of active pastors are divorced.
- 23% have been fired or pressured to resign from their church at least once.

- 25% don't know where to turn when they have a family or personal conflict or issue.
- 25% of pastors' spouses see their mate's work schedule as a source of conflict.
- 33% felt burned out within their first five years of ministry.
- 33% say that being in ministry is an outright hazard to their family.
- 40% of pastors and 47% of spouses are suffering from burnout, frantic schedules, and/or unrealistic expectations.
- 45% of pastors' wives say the greatest danger to them and their family is physical, emotional, mental, and spiritual burnout.
- 45% of pastors say that they have experienced depression or burnout to the extent that they needed to take a leave of absence from ministry.
- 50% feel unable to meet the needs of the job.
- 52% of pastors say they and their spouses believe that being in pastoral ministry is hazardous to their family's well-being and health.
- 56% of pastors' wives say that they have no close friends.
- 57% would leave the pastorate if they had somewhere else to go or some other vocation they could do.
- 70% don't have any close friends.
- 75% report severe stress causing anguish, worry, bewilderment, anger, depression, fear, and alienation.

- 80% of pastors say they have insufficient time with their spouse.
- 80% believe that pastoral ministry affects their families negatively.
- 90% work more than 50 hours a week.
- 94% feel under pressure to have a perfect family.
- 1,500 pastors leave their ministries each month due to burnout, conflict, or moral failure.[19]
- 50% of all congregations in the United States are either plateauing or declining.
- 33% of pastors confess "inappropriate" sexual behavior with someone in the church.
- 75% report they have had a significant stress-related crisis at least once in their ministry.
- 90% feel inadequately trained to cope with ministry demands.
- 40% report a serious conflict with a parishioner at least once a month.[20]
- Among all degreed professionals in the U. S., pastors are the lowest paid, averaging $28,000.00 per year in income. One out of five pastors has to work a second job to support himself and his family.[21]

---

[19] Daniel Sherman, "Statistics on Pastor Burnout," *PastorBurnout.com* (publication date unknown). Accessed on October 22, 2014.

[20] H. B. London Jr. and Neil B. Wiseman, *Pastors at Greater Risk* (Ventura CA: Gospel Light Publications, 2003), 20-21.

[21] Jack Wellman, "Average Pastor Salaries in United States Churches," *Patheos* (December 15 2014). Accessed on January 3, 2015.

Again, the high number of recent clergy suicides in a culture where numerous signs indicate that many more are in trouble is alarming and poses a major problem going forward. These statistics and other studies show that rates of depression and dissatisfaction among clergy are at an all-time high. The culture of burnout, hopelessness, and fatigue coupled with a lack of clergy support systems for those who are battling depression or who are in trouble alert us that unless we change the church culture more suicides are on the horizon.

Greg Warner's article on clergy suicide in *USA Today*, for example, addressed the obstacles pastors face in today's church culture.

> Those who counsel pastors say Christian culture, especially Southern evangelicalism, creates the perfect environment for depression. Pastors suffer in silence, unwilling or unable to seek help or even talk about it. Sometimes they leave ministry. Occasionally the result is unthinkable.[22]

---

[22] Greg Warner, "Suicide: When pastors' silent suffering turns tragic," *USAToday.com* (October 29, 2009). Accessed on September 18, 2014.

Clergy are very vulnerable because there are risk factors for clergy that other professions do not have. In professions like entertainment, education, business, government, and medicine, employers offer support and leave time for mental health issues. After people receive treatment, they can return to work. This is not the case in most churches. Many parishioners still do not believe that good pastors can struggle from mental illness or addictions. They reason, "If they are holy enough and have enough faith, everything will be fine." Beliefs such as this drive clergy into secrecy.

Where do troubled clergy turn? How many churches will give them a leave of absence, financial and emotional support through difficult times? Whom can clergy seek out for counsel or safely tell their secrets? What systems are in place to help them?

The truth is there are few denominational or para-church recovery programs for clergy with addictions. Many churches do not provide money for pastors to see a therapist or seek other forms of mental health assistance. Far too few pastors can step away from their duties for a period to address emotional, psychological, or familial challenges. The church has a long way to go in this area and we need to start building bridges with the mental health community and educating our churches about mental health.

With a culture of congregational dysfunction in which a precedent has been set, even more pastors may turn to self-destruction. Pastors who feel isolated and beyond help or think their families and churches will be better off without them, may follow their colleagues down the dark path to suicide. Since the news of Rev. Parker's death in November 2014, for example, at least twelve more pastors have committed suicide. We do not know if there is a correlation between increased publicity regarding clergy suicides and the increased number of clergy who recently committed suicide. Yet, it is important to pay attention.

There may be a correlation between the obsession with church growth and rising rates of clergy dysfunction. The obsession, in small to medium sized churches, pushes pastors and leaders to make their church the next mega-church, the next big thing in the community or state. This puts these pastors at-risk for burnout, depression, divorce, and now suicide. This culture of growth as the primary – and for some, the only – marker of success is doing more harm than good.

Churches often frame their desire to grow membership in evangelistic terms. Yet, authentic evangelism does not always translate into larger congregations. American Protestantism has lost its way by obsessing over having big and more, being bigger and even more, or the biggest and most. This monster is devouring pastors and their families.

Pastors are going and going and going, all in the name of the church's new obsession for growth, for a big church, a bigger church, then the biggest church. Pastors are preaching multiple services, some at multiple locations, and some in different states. Yet, this culture has nothing to do with souls. Within many of the bigger and biggest churches, nominalism is rampant and authentic discipleship died decades ago. Too many contemporary Christians are content to go to church, and could not care less about being a disciple of Jesus Christ. The megachurches they attend are cultural markers of success and achievement; they have become hallmarks of the triumph of a capitalist and consumerist religion.

The worst manifestation of this obsession with growth is the tendency to treat clergy in utilitarian ways.

Some believe that a good action or end is one that helps the greatest number of people. Churches become utilitarian when congregations, denominations, and ministry organizations use pastors in whatever way they deem good to help themselves stay financially viable.

This approach to ministry comes at a great cost for clergy who are viewed as dispensable commodities. In return for prominence and financial well-being, they surrender talent, energy, time, and family. Their gifts are used and reused until they are used up. Then pastors become disposable resources to be discarded. If they lose their drawing power, they are deemed less valuable. Older preachers can be replaced by younger ones. Divorced preachers can be replaced by newly married ones. Less dynamic preachers can be replaced by ones that are more dynamic.

With the plethora of divinity schools, seminaries, Bible colleges, and church schools turning out potential leaders, it is easy to discard troubled clergy – to expose, fire, and displace the man or woman who has given so much. It is not surprising, then, that many clergy feel of little use to a church when they are physically or mentally ill, depressed or involved in misconduct. They adequately represent the culture of today's church. As long as clergy are of use and have value to a congregation or denomination, they can stay and lead. If their value decreases in some way, churches have a way of telling them they are no longer useful. For there is no shortage of ministers waiting in the wings for their turn to be the pastor.

We rarely talk about this side of ministry in popular media. Instead, the discussions about abuse and misconduct are, often, one-sided, focusing exclusively on clergy behavior. Truthfully, however, congregations are also, sometimes, abusive and denominational systems can exploit and misuse clergy. Some addictions and misconduct prevalent among clergy result from years of abuse at the hand of the church. Clergy who feel abused and discarded are prime candidates for dysfunctional behaviors, including suicide. This is especially true when they have been spurned by the church, exiled to obscurity within the community, and labelled as one who "used to pastor a church."

Conclusion

Where do we go from here? The issue is serious and we are seeing only the tip of an iceberg. Denominational leaders, seminary faculties and others interested in the health of the church must seriously address clergy suicide.

First, we need to gather detailed data on clergy suicide. We need to know about the demographics of those who take this way out. How many cases of suicide have occurred in the last two decades? What are the demographics: racial-ethnic and gender status, denominational affiliation, and geographical regions of the country? What are the circumstances surrounding their deaths? Such information can help denominational leaders, seminaries, clergy, and churches to grasp the scope of the problem.

We need data on the effectiveness of strategies congregations employed to cope with pastoral suicide. What sermons were preached at the funeral service? What was done to help church members and others in the community cope with the crisis? To what extent and how effectively did the churches turn to mental health professionals to process the trauma and grief. What theological questions did parishioners raise about suicide?

It would be especially important to determine how these congregations sought to interpret these tragic events. Which biblical texts did they draw on? What questions did the pastor's suicide raise about their church's approach to ministry? Did theological beliefs about faith and prayer conflict with mental health issues? What changes, if any, have churches made following a former pastor's suicide? How are these congregations faring today and what are the residual effects?

These questions will yield rich material for further reflection and developing long-range strategies. A study of this magnitude may take a year or longer to complete. Yet, it is imperative that it happen, for currently we do not have enough data to ascertain what needs to be done.

Second, there are specific areas that need to be addressed. As Parker's death illustrates, there is clear evidence that untreated depression can lead to suicide. We, therefore, need not have a simplistic, monolithic conversation about such a complex issue. We must talk about how the larger issues of clergy health contribute to or guard against suicide.

Further, we must talk about the susceptibility of clergy family members to suicide since there are signs that this may be a problem for them as well. In this work, three suicides we have discussed involved members of clergy families.

We also need to discuss clergy misconduct as a major factor in the turn to suicide, though not all clergy who are involved in misconduct commit suicide. Yet, how are the two issues related? Is misconduct a predictor of a possible suicide attempt or an indicator of the type of emotional or moral instability that would leave one vulnerable to attempting suicide?

This discussion has to happen on two levels. We need to hold clergy involved in misconduct accountable. Further, those who are on the verge of a congregational, denominational, and possibly a legal action also need to be accountable while we support their rehabilitation. Discarding, dismissing, and alienating fallen pastors only increases the chance they may commit suicide. What they need from the church is help to find hope for moral recovery. They need to regain a vision of their life beyond the immediate misconduct. They do not need to be let off the hook for actions that have tainted theirs and other people's lives, but they must be given the possibility of reconciliation and regaining their usefulness to the faith community.

At the same time, if there are increased cases of clergy misconduct, we will need more conversations about moral accountability. This may signal the need for increased education about boundaries and the fallout misconduct brings to everyone involved. We need to raise the church's awareness of these issues, change the culture of congregations, and find ways to support clergy families caught in these situations.

This urgent issue demands an immediate response from all major stakeholders -- pastors, congregational and denominational leaders, mental health professionals, and seminary and divinity school faculties. Then it is imperative that we disseminate this information as we develop comprehensive strategies for an issue that will not go away, but threatens to grow within ever more challenging ministry contexts.

Rather than a private or local issue, clergy suicide has national impact and demands a concerted, national response – a national awareness campaign. I am sounding the first alarm as a step toward making the faith community aware of the tragedy of increasing clergy suicide among us.

But awareness is only a first step. For beyond awareness, making progress in the area of mental health it is imperative that the faith community develops a cogent, persuasive theology that refuses to condemn ministers who struggle with depression and other forms of mental illness – especially those who become victims of suicide. This theology must take seriously the realities of the human condition – that we are all subject to outworking of our sinful, human nature. Further, we are all in need of the atoning work of Christ on our half and in need of the forgiveness that atonement provides, regardless of how that sinful nature may manifest itself.

This theology has to be willing to deal biblically with the hard questions regarding suicide and cannot be based on outdated, biblical misconceptions regarding the ability of Christ's atoning work and that forgiveness to avail itself even for those Christians who find themselves in a position of being unable to ask for it.

4 Suicide: The Unpardonable Sin?

The belief that suicide victims go to hell is widespread, and pervasive among many in the Evangelical church. Often when the tragedy of suicide rears its ugly head in the church, such a contention complicates the grieving process, and prolongs the course of healing for those who are left behind.

The last funeral I attended as pastor of a small, Louisville, Kentucky congregation involved the suicide of a young man. The family and community were reeling because of this death. Their grief was intensified by was the belief among many in the congregation that this young man went to hell because he committed suicide. This belief was so pervasive that the eulogist felt compelled to address it. The unfortunate choice for that conversation in this inappropriate venue only made matters worse.

While I applaud his courage in challenging this deeply held conviction on the part of that congregation, his wisdom in choosing this venue to explore the complexities of this issue is questionable. Yet, in truth, the church needs to have this discussion before another suicide occurs. This attitude short-circuits the church's attempt to respond to suicide victims and their families, compounding their grief in unfortunate ways. It creates tension among families, churches, and communities and generates one of two responses – neither are helpful. People either feel sorry for the victim and their family or they harshly judge them based on a theology that, ironically, has no basis in Scripture.

Such beliefs complicate the grieving process for families and congregations after the suicidal death of a pastor. For example, after Parker's death, his close friend, Dr. E. Dewey Smith and Dr. Steven Land addressed the belief that a person who commits suicide goes to hell. For example, these are two comments publicly posted on the Christian Post's Facebook page after Parker's death. One person said, "Sorry but anyone who takes their own life is not resting in peace. He's a coward, instead of getting on his knees, like a real Christian. He took his own life." Another person added, "Very sad my brother lost the fight… the race is not for the swift nor the battle for the strong but it is for those who endure to the end... nobody can put you into heaven after committing such an act sorry!!!!" [23]

Smith and Land both criticized the insensitive and unbiblical nature of such assertions. Smith was interviewed by the Christian Post and claimed that Parker was sick, not immoral. He retorted, "Is it fair to blame a victim for being sick?" He was saddened by the mean and hurtful comments that pervaded the world of social media after his death. Land was also interviewed and said this belief is unbiblical. He added, "The position that suicide somehow would cancel your salvation has no biblical support whatsoever. When it is a result of mental illness it is not a sin. Sins are when you knowingly do things that are contrary to God's will and that involves rational thought processes and choices. A person who is in the midst of a tremendous depression for instance, is not a rational person."[24] I commend Drs. Smith and Land for challenging this belief but this article only underscores the need to challenge this belief because many Christians have not been taught on this subject.

---

[23] Leonardo Blair, "Belief That Pastor Who Killed Himself Is Going to Hell Is 'Ludicrous' and 'Unbiblical,' Say Dr. Richard Land, Pastor E. Dewey Smith," (November 14, 2013). Accessed on September 20, 2014.

[24] Ibid.

This belief is widespread among many Christians and influences the insensitive attitudes people hold regarding the eternal fare of those who have committed suicide. They don't help develop theologies and strategies that help families and congregations deal with the loss. In many instances, they are hypocritical.

The Church and the Sanctity of All Life: Two Case Studies

In one sense, the Church's hypocrisy regarding the issue of suicide specifically relates to the belief in the sanctity of life, since it holds that suicide dishonors that sanctity. Interestingly, however, we do not always consider this sanctity in its broader terms.

If life is sacred, to be protected at all costs, there are implications for all life and health choices. This valuing cannot not be selectively employed for choices with which we do not agree or areas to which we are not particularly susceptible.

Some Christians are exceptionally harsh in condemning a person who commits suicide but not for those who knowingly do things that cause death to themselves in other ways. While we know that smoking is intensely harmful to the body in many ways, some Christians smoke until they get lung cancer. Others, who are fully aware of the hazards of obesity, overeat until they have diabetes and heart problems. When these people die, there is rarely similar condemnation coming from the church.

A pastor can drive his luxury sedan at a high speed, losing control of it and die while possibly killing others. Members of the congregation will treat that death as an accident, convincing themselves it was not intentional. While intention is important, however, genuine respect for the sanctity of life is equally important. The pastor is not respecting life's sanctity when illegally driving a dangerous motor vehicle at such high speeds.

Does killing oneself instantly substantially differ from killing oneself gradually or "accidentally"? Why does the church focus on and condemn one and not the other, if sanctity of life is really the issue? Two case studies illustrate the tension the church faces regarding these issues.

Case 1: Old Jim.

Old Jim was a familiar fixture in the community. Everybody knew him and he knew almost everybody and about everything going on in town. A drive through town was not complete without a wave or passing word to Jim. He was a warm and friendly soul. He would give candy to kids and help mothers with grocery bags. Old Jim would talk football and politics at the town barbershop with the guys. He even did a little mechanic work for folks. The highlight of the year was Jim's practice of dressing up as Santa Claus for the community Christmas party.

  The kids enjoyed Jim making promises that moms and dads in town had to keep. The local pastor of the Baptist Church always marveled at Jim for his love and warmth. He lived out his faith in ways that touched many lives.

  One Tuesday afternoon Jim's granddaughter, Sallie, was tragically killed in a car accident while Jim was driving the car. He had promised to pick up Sallie from ballet practice. Though Jim had been drinking and had become intoxicated, he kept his promise. In his impaired state, he ran off the road and slammed into a tree; killing Sallie instantly, but he survived.

  The news of Sallie's death devastated the small town, and Jim was inconsolable. The family received many acts of graciousness including phone calls, cards, and hot meals for the parents of the young girl and for Jim. The church held a large funeral and helped with burial expenses.

He shut himself in his home and neighbors could hear him loudly crying for hours. Jim's grief was so deep that on the day of Sallie's funeral, he killed himself. Not only was a young girl's life lost, but so was that of her grandfather. The family, the congregation, and the town suffered two deep tragedies.

Since the church held that people who commit suicide go to hell, the congregation was even more distraught. Many believed that Jim's life of good deeds counted for nothing because of the way he died. Some openly talked about Jim being in hell for committing suicide. The church voted not to hold Jim's funeral. Instead, Jim's family, who had suffered two inconsolable losses back to back, was left to bear the burden and grief of the second one alone. Even worse, they had to hear insensitive remarks regarding the circumstances of his death and were forced to hold a small memorial service in the local funeral home and few of the congregation attended.

Case 2. Aunt Mays

Aunt Mays was one of the old faithful mothers of the Holiness Church in the county. She rarely missed a worship service, coming early on Sunday morning and being among the last to leave mid-week prayer service. Yet while she was faithful, many kids at the church considered her downright hateful. She yelled at them and gave mean looks in worship, often threatening to take a switch to them if she felt they were misbehaving.

Aunt Mays was a legend in church for her appetite. At one church dinner last year she ate eight pieces of chicken and two plates of macaroni and cheese, not counting the biscuits. One month she won first place in pie eating contest at the county fair. She beat Randy, a three-time champion, by a pie and a half. It was quite a scene watching her put that food away.

Yes Aunt Mays was somebody you loved one minute and hated the next. It was a tough time at Solid Rock Holiness Church when everyone found out that she died of congestive heart failure. It seemed like everybody came to her funeral, either to pay their respects or see her extra-large casket. That day was a spectacle as the large crowd gathered.

The pastor preached an inspiring message. He said Aunt Mays had gone on to heaven – to her eternal reward.

The very different manner in which these churches made the connection between sin and death shows how our understanding of the connection is worked out when death either comes immediately versus when it comes gradually, even if the person who dies is, at least in part, the perpetrator. Clearly, there is the profound hypocrisy in the church regarding the issue of the sanctity of life that arises from a key theological understanding of self-murder as sin that undergirds the misguided belief that Christians who commit suicide die in sin and go to hell.

These fictional cases illustrate the reality that many churches shun families whose loved one dies by suicide while they celebrate the life of a "good" person who dies by what they consider "natural causes," even when that death is hastened by decades of poor health choices. Do we have to shun one and not the other? Can we embrace and minister to both families? What can we do debunk a popular belief that is held by many Christians?

We must first understand that this belief is drawn from inaccurate scriptural inferences that feed erroneous beliefs about the effect of human decisions on a person's salvation or eternal state. There are three inferences that support this belief: suicide is murder, it is a breach of the sanctity of life and the sovereignty of God over life, and a person who commits suicide dies with unconfessed sin.

While Christians may agree on the sinfulness of suicide, attitudes regarding the implications of this action on a person's eternal standing with God vary. Plainly, self-killing or self-murder is a clear breach of one of the Ten Commandments. The Bible teaches that life is a gift from God because life comes from God. Christians, therefore hold that all life is sacred, and see the issue of ending a life as such a serious and controversial matter. Those who believe that people who commit suicide go to hell contend that this person not only ends a life that is sacred, but acts in the place of God who has the sovereign right over life and death. Hebrews 9:27 states, "It is appointed to humans once to die but after that the judgment."

That appointment is understood as having been made by God who has the sovereign right to decide when a person dies, not them. Therefore, suicide breaches God's right to decide the time of death. When one kills him or herself, they usurp the right that God holds as creator of all life. Those who hold this view conclude, therefore, the person who dies having broken the Commandment against killing while usurping God's sovereignty over life dies "in sin" and is eternally condemned. For this group, suicide is an unpardonable sin – a special class of sin with irreversible eternal consequences.

This belief is problematic for many reasons. First, the belief that suicide is an unpardonable sin is inconsistent with the teachings of Scripture on salvation. Suicide apparently rules out one's profession of faith in Jesus Christ and his redemptive work on the cross for the sins of humanity. Such reasoning runs contrary to foundational texts that speak of salvation as a gift from God.

> *For it is by grace that you have been saved through faith and this not from yourselves, it is a gift from God- not by works, so that no one can boast.* (Eph. 2:8-9)

> *That if you confess with your mouth, "Jesus is Lord,"and believe in your heart that God raised him from the dead, you will be saved. For it is with your heart that you believe and are justified, and it is with your mouth that you confess and are saved. As the Scripture says, "Anyone who*

> *trusts in him will never be put to shame…For "Everyone who calls on the name of the Lord will be saved."* (Rom. 10:9-11, 13)

It is consistent that we are saved by grace through faith rather than by our works (Eph 2:8) yet many Christians insist that suicide cancels the gift of salvation. Though heartfelt belief and open confession of faith in Christ Jesus assures us of salvation (Rom 10:9-11), some contend that the singular act of suicide nullifies one's faith and confession, such that the Romans text should read if you believe on the name of the Lord, and do not commit suicide you shall be saved.

This belief has no biblical support among the seven accounts of suicide recorded in Scripture. Abimelech was severely injured by a woman and ordered his armor bearer to kill him, which is a form of an assisted suicide (Judges 9:54). Samson killed himself by killing three thousand Philistines who were on the roof of a house that collapsed on everyone (Judges 16:30). Saul killed himself in a battle with the Philistines instead of being killed by his enemies (1 Samuel 31:4). Saul's armor bearer killed himself after seeing his king commit suicide (1 Samuel 31:5). Ahithophel was so disgusted over the collapse of his influence with King David that he went home, set his affairs in order, and hanged himself (2 Sam 17:23). Zimri who saw that Israel was being overrun, went into the palace and burnt it down while he was in it and died (1 Kgs 16:18). Finally, Judas Iscariot who betrayed Jesus to the Romans, was distraught over his actions and hung himself (27:3-10 and Acts 1:16-20). The Bible does not ever suggest that any of these people were condemned to hell because of their actions. The important factor in the death of these biblical characters is not how they died as much as how they lived.

In Sampson's specific case, it is difficult to make the case for his condemnation since, after his death by suicide, the book of Hebrews lists him as an exemplar of faith.

> *And what more shall I say? I do not have time to tell about Gideon, Barak, Samson, Jephthah, David, Samuel and the Prophets, who through faith conquered kingdoms, administered justice, and gained what was promised; who shut the mouths of lions, quenched the fury of the flames, and escaped the edge of the sword;* **whose weakness was turned to strength**; *and who became powerful in battle and routed foreign armies.* (Heb. 11:32-34)

The reference to Samson's weakness turning to strength is a clear allusion to his death in Judges 16. After Delilah finally seduced him into revealing the secret of his strength[25] she called for a man to shave off the seven braids of his hair. After the Philistines captured him, they gouged out his eyes and their rulers gathered for a celebration to Dagon, the Philistine god, who had delivered Samson to them. They were celebrating a major victory and shouting, "bring out Samson to entertain us" (16:25). Importantly, as Israel's once mighty judge was blind, performing for the Philistines, the following scene unfolded:

> *When they stood him among the pillars, Samson said to the servant who held his hand, "Put me where I can feel the pillars that support the temple, so that I may lay against them." Now the temple was crowded with men and women watching Samson perform. Then Samson prayed to the Lord, O sovereign Lord, remember me. O God, please strengthen me just once more, and let me with one blow get revenge on the Philistines for my two eyes. Then Samson reached toward the two central pillars on which the temple stood. Bracing himself against them, his right hand on one*

---

[25] No razor had ever been used on his head because he was under a Nazarite vow from birth (see Judges 13:3-5).

> *and his left hand on the other, Samson said, Let me die with the Philistines! Then he pushed with all his might, and down came the temple on the rulers and all the people in it. Thus he killed many more when he died than while he lived.* (Jdg. 16:25b-30)

The account of his death by suicide clearly shows the author does not condemn him for his ignominious death. In fact, one could argue that the narrative of his death portrays him as an imperfect hero who does one final act of good for the children of Israel by killing more Philistines in his death than he did in his life. The point in referring the listing of his name in Hebrews and the Judges 16 account of his suicide is to raise a question. Why include Samson in Hebrews 11 as an exemplar of faith if he was eternally lost because of his actions? The obvious answer is that he was included because the Bible does not correlate suicide with being damned to hell. However, this misguided belief persists in too many churches.

Not only is this belief inconsistent with the Bible, it is inconsistent with Christian theology because it creates a special classification of sin. Suicide becomes a singular sin with eternal consequences, that "supposedly" can cancel out a life of faith and, ultimately, one's salvation while "lesser" sins – lying, lust, hatred, jealousy, malice, envy, wrath, greed, unforgiveness, and strife – do not. A Christian can lie to a nurse about taking medication, die of a heart attack, and go to heaven, but if that same Christian commits suicide and dies, he or she is hell bound. For some reason, suicide is a special class of sin.

Moreover, we must ask why suicide is treated in this manner, as a special type of sin? Again, theological understandings of death complicate the answer. The issue of death raises eschatological questions about meaning in life. What happens when temporal life ends? How does the manner in which we live correlate with what happens to us after death? But a foundational question for Evangelical Christians is related to unconfessed sin.

Some presume that the act of suicide has significant consequences on our eternal standing before God because the person who kills him or herself has no opportunity to receive forgiveness for this unconfessed sin. This final act creates a problem that can only be solved by a righteous God assigning them to hell. Accordingly, the deeper issue is dying, having committed a sin considered murder and not having the chance to seek forgiveness for an unconfessed sin.

Forgiveness and its Ambiguous Role on Salvation

Much of the confusion stems from a misunderstanding regarding God's ability and willingness to forgive and its relation to salvation. If a person has to seek pardon for very individual sin, then the circumstances of suicide do not allow opportunity to do what is necessary to receive forgiveness.

Forgiveness is a dominant theme in relation to salvation. When the angel announced to Mary that she would bring forth the Christ child, the angel told her that his name would be Jesus for he shall save his people from their sins.[26] Jesus came to offer forgiveness of sins for all people. That is why forgiveness a major theme of the New Testament.

> *Peter replied, repent and be baptized, every one of you, in the name of Jesus Christ for the forgiveness of sins. And you will receive the gift of the Holy Spirit.* (Acts 2:38)

---

[26] Matt. 1:21.

Texts such as Acts 2:38 suggest that experiencing salvation means receiving the pardon from one's sins as necessary when one stands before God in Judgment. According to the Hebrews' text, Jesus' sacrificial death has atoned for our sins and made our righteous standing possible. Those who believe in Jesus Christ and confess him as savior will be saved. For those in Christ are forgiven for past, present, and future sins so that we will experience eternal fellowship with God. Those who have not been forgiven will stand condemned before God.

Some Christians remain unable to understand the relation between the forgiveness of sins committed after conversion and their effect on one's salvation. They think of salvation exclusively in terms of the forgiveness of sin, and the issue of the relation of forgiveness and salvation looms large in their minds as they seek to make sense of the tragedy of suicide.

In fact, suicide raises this question but it extends to every Christian who dies "in sin" or with unconfessed sins. Can such a Christian go to heaven if they die in a state of spiritual estrangement from God or does one have to faithful until the moment of death?

Further probing questions may help clarify the issue. Is it possible that one has to ask forgiveness for every sin or will God forgive even if one does not ask for it? Is it necessary to name specific sins when asking for forgiveness or can we make a general petition for forgiveness? What if certain sins are intentionally or accidentally omitted from our request – is our eternal standing before God affected? There is ambiguity around these issues that opens the door, for the contention that belief that the one commits suicide is destined for hell. However, it does not prove this belief.

The New Testament is clear that we should confess our sins, but does it teach that our salvation is dependent on our petitioning for all our sins to be forgiven? Jesus taught his disciples to seek for forgiveness when they prayed to the Father in heaven.[27] Yet, there aren't that many New Testament passages regarding the practice. Among the few are,

> *Be kind and compassionate to one another, forgiving each other, just as Christ God forgave you.* (Eph. 4:32)

or

---

[27] Matt. 6:12 and Mk. 11:25-26.

> *Therefore confess your sins to each other and pray for each other that you may be healed.* (Jas. 5:16)

Most texts regarding forgiveness, focus on forgiving one another of sins and one text focuses on confessing one's sin to God:

> *If we confess our sins he is faithful and just to forgive us our sins and purify us from all unrighteousness.* (1 Jn. 1:9)

In the Ephesians and James texts, one does not ask God but rather confesses sin to a fellow Christian. The texts in James and 1 John may imply the need to be specific about the sins we confess but no text says it is required. The New Testament does not teach that one's salvation is dependent on the confession of every sin. Rather, it simply instructs Christians to confess their sins.

Seeking forgiveness is important but not salvific. It is essential for maintaining intimate fellowship with God, as well as communal and familial relationships. Christians do not have to log and keep track of sins to ensure they cover them all in petitions for forgiveness.

Forgiveness serves an essential function. In James, praying for forgiveness brings healing. There is a similar idea found in Paul's discourse on the Lord's Supper. He instructs those who partake of the bread and cup to "examine ourselves (1 Cor. 11:28)." The implication is to look at oneself honestly and earnestly and at the intention of our heart, not in making sure every sin is accounted for.

In these texts, what is important is an attitude and disposition before God that speaks of humble dependence of God for salvation, not one's ability to keep God's commands perfectly.

Most texts regarding forgiveness deal with human relationships. This being a particular concern of Jesus in the gospels suggests that God is more concerned with that than keeping track of sin. The one exception, of course, is 1 John 1:9 that says "if we confess our sins (God) is faithful and just to forgive us our sins and cleanse us from all unrighteousness." This is a clear reference to the practice of asking God for forgiveness but the text or the larger 1 John passage does not, in any way, require the continued confession of individual sins. John assumes, that instead of pretending one has no sin, our confession that we are sinners who need continually to be cleansed from all unrighteousness is recognition of our implicit sinfulness.

Indeed, Scripture places greater emphasis on repentance. In the messages to the seven churches in the book of Revelation, Jesus commends churches for specific good deeds and rebukes churches for specific sins. Afterwards, he charges them to repent – not ask for forgiveness – and warns churches that a failure to repent brings judgment.

Jesus told the church at Ephesus he would remove their lampstand from its place (Rev. 2:5). He told the church at Pergamum he would war against them with the sword of his mouth (Rev. 2:16). He told the church at Thyatira he would throw them on a sickbed and into tribulation (Rev. 2:22). He told the church at Sardis he would blot his name out of the book of life (Rev. 3:5). He told the church at Laodicea that he would spew them out of his mouth (Rev. 3:16). While these punishments are severe, with the possible exception of the warning given to the church at Sardis, none seem to suggest an eternity in hell. This is significant, especially considering a later judgment passage in chapter twenty.

> *The dead were judged according to what they had done as recorded in the books. The sea gave up the dead that were in it, and death and Hades gave up the dead that were in it, and death and Hades gave up the dead that were in them, and each person was judged according to what he had done. Then death and Hades were thrown into the lake of fire. The lake of fire is the second death. If anyone's name was not found written in the book of life, he was thrown into the lake of fire.* (Rev. 20:12b-15)

Such warnings may imply a need to acknowledge a specific sin or transgression and repent – turn away from it. While they provide evidence of the importance of being forgiven for a sin before it merits a divine response of some kind, but it is a stretch to view such texts as a universal requirement. More importantly, again, one could argue that the focus in Revelation is not forgiveness but repentance.

The New Testament is silent on the final issue of unconfessed sin. This vague term, "unconfessed sin," can mean a variety of things and carries assumptions on which Christians disagree. Those who dismiss this understanding of a need to confess specific sins would argue that a sincere petition for forgiveness will suffice.

The New Testament does not outline what God will do about sins we have not confessed and asked for forgiveness by the time of death. Furthermore, the Bible makes no assertion that unconfessed sin nullifies a person's position as a child of God.

God's merciful and gracious actions on behalf of Christians who commit suicide is independent of their ability to obey God perfectly. In sins of omission or commission, God shows grace because of the perfect work of Christ. Scripture is not silent about the ability of that work to affect salvation from both the power of sin and our individual sins.

More to Salvation than Forgiveness of Sins

While the forgiveness of sins is an important part of any understanding of salvation, there are additional ways to talk about salvation. The New Testament provides rich and varied language to talk about salvation that goes beyond the forgiveness of sins. And it is important to view the issue of suicide through the broader lens of the New Testament's teaching on salvation:

1). Redemption. To redeem means to buy back and suggests that Christ's sacrificial death paid the entire price or penalty for all our sin. Believers are redeemed by Christ from the power of sin and the dominion of darkness.

For all have sinned and fall short of the glory of God, and are justified freely by his grace through the redemption that came by Christ Jesus. (Rom. 3:23-24)

...In him we have redemption through his blood. (Eph. 1:7 and Col. 1:13-14)

2). Regeneration. This term suggests being born-again from above. Regeneration speaks to the transformational dimensions of salvation made possible by the indwelling presence and power of the Holy Spirit. Before salvation, believers were dead in sin. This means they were spiritually dead, lacking the life-giving, indwelling presence of the Holy Spirit. At conversion, believers are made alive in Christ and experience a second birth called regeneration.

He saved us, not because of righteous things we have done, but because of his mercy. He saved us through the washing of rebirth and renewal by the Holy Spirit, whom he poured out on us generously through Jesus Christ our Lord. (Tit. 3:5)

I tell you the truth, no one can see the kingdom of God unless he is born again...Jesus answered I tell you the truth no one can enter the kingdom of God unless he is born of water and the Spirit. Flesh gives birth to flesh but spirit gives birth to spirit. (Jn. 3:3, 5-7)

3). Adoption. The term adoption signifies that at conversion, the believer is brought into the family of God as a full member with full rights and privileges. The person who was formerly not a member of God's family, becomes an heir with Jesus Christ – God's only *begotten* Son – of all that God has in store.

For you did not receive a spirit that makes you a slave again to fear, but you received the Spirit of sonship. And by him we cry, "Abba, Father." The Spirit himself testifies with our spirit that we are God's children. Now if we are children, then we are heirs- heirs of God and co-heirs with Christ. (Rom. 8:15-17a)

But when the time had fully come, God sent his Son, born of a woman, born under law, to redeem those under law, that we might receive the full rights of sons. Because you are sons, God sent the Spirit of his Son into our hearts, the Spirit who calls out "Abba, Father." So you are no longer a slave, but a son; and since you are a son, God made you also an heir. (Gal. 4:4-7)

4). Justification. This is the concept of being declared or made righteous. It is a legal and juridical act whereby God declares the believing sinner to be righteous in Jesus Christ. He removes guilt, imputes the righteousness of Christ to us, and treats us *just as if* that sin never happened.

Where then is boasting? It is excluded. On what principle? On that of observing the law? No, but on that of faith. For we maintain that a man is justified by faith apart from observing the law. (Rom. 3:27-28)

These concepts provide a fuller description of God's salvific work in Jesus Christ. While the issue of forgiveness is important, it is just as important to discuss the implications of suicide for believers who have been redeemed, regenerated, adopted, and justified by God because of what Jesus Christ accomplished in his death and resurrection.

Their misguided, faithless, and even sinful act of taking their own lives is not able to undo what God definitively did in Jesus two thousand years ago on Calvary's cross.

The Sufficiency of Christ to Save

The New Testament writers were convinced that those who are in Christ are saved "by grace through faith and not works." Their conviction was that the one who saves is Jesus. Jesus made salvation possible and He is sufficient to carry out his saving work to completion, including the moment of coming to faith, the life of faith, and the future day of salvation when all things culminate in him. What gets lost with the belief that a person who commits suicide goes to hell is the belief in the sufficiency of Jesus Christ to save. The teachings of the New Testament support the belief that the atoning work Jesus Christ is also adequate to save them.

The New Testament speaks to the sufficiency of Christ for anyone who dies with unconfessed sin, including people who die by suicide. There are helpful reminders of God's faithfulness, God's promises, and God's power to effect salvation found within its pages. First, Jesus, our High Priest, makes intercession to the Father on our behalf (Heb.

4:14-16; 7:25-26). Because of this, Jesus intercedes for believers who die by suicide. There is no reason, then, to believe their actions cancel out their salvation.

When Christians sin we have an advocate – a helper – with the Father, Jesus Christ the Righteous One, the covering of our sin and sins (1 Jn. 2:1-2). Jesus serves as an advocate for Christians who commit suicide, as well as all other Christians and all other sins. In their ultimate state of weakness, he helps them and his death covers their sin, even the sin of self-killing.

Jesus is the one who keeps those in Christ from falling in the ultimate sense and is the one who presents them faultless before God (Jude 24-25). Jesus will present suicide victims before the throne of God on the day of the Lord without fault. He can do this because he has sufficiently atoned for their sins and they are righteous in him, not in themselves.

The Bible is clear that nothing -- not even death nor any other thing in creation – can separate Christians from the love of God, (Rom. 8:37-39). Even in the painful depths of death brought on by suicide, God's love persists and stays with us, not allowing even death to separate them from his love.

Because Christ's work is sufficient, the manner of death should not be the focal point in any discussion about one's eternal destiny because saving lost souls is the work of God, not humans. The reality that Jesus died for our sins, saved us from our sins, and pleads our case before God, is sufficient for both confessed sin as well as unconfessed sin. People who are in Christ are completely covered because his work is sufficient to save. Failure to request forgiveness for a final sin cannot cancel out this work.

Conclusion

In the end, we must develop theologies that speak to mental illness and suicide. We must challenge any theology of sin that eclipses God's love that comes to us as the gospel of Jesus Christ or of salvation that centralizes human responsibility to the moment of death. This is not only bad theology for those who commit suicide, it is bad theology for the church!

The church must, further, expand its understanding of the sanctity life as a gift from God and all forms of self-killing behavior as abhorrent. Jumping off bridges, poor health choices, and violence within our communities must be denounced as self-destructive behavior that cannot be tolerated.

We have to speak a word of comfort and hope for families and congregations that have been traumatized by clergy suicide. For, if, as the Bible teaches, "Nothing shall separate us from the love of God" (Rom. 8:39), this includes the death that we bring on ourselves.

When a loved one commits suicide, survivors are left with many thoughts and emotions including guilt that they did not recognize the signs or may have contributed to the suicide in some way, loneliness, or even anger. Further, there may be guilt associated with the fact that there is anger. Surviving spouses and families lose their social bearing. They do not understand where they fit or are forced out of a spiritual community that was once their special place – their home. What authentic comfort can we offer them?

Finally, we need to challenge religious and social structures that rob millions – even millions of Christians of hope and the realization of the abundant life that Christ came to give. We, who call ourselves by the name of Christ, must denounce all life destroying forces within our communities including the drive for unrealistic success, the push to perfection, alienation for authentic human relationships, and the greed for power. These forces lead to the hopeless despair that fosters self-destroying attitudes and behaviors.

There is much work required to understand the intersection of issues that lead troubled pastors to turn to suicide. What makes the men and women to whom we traditionally turn to help us through our troubled times, themselves turn to such drastic measures. What are the lies that keep leaders from seeking more effective solutions?

We must move away from believing that moral perfection is required for entry to heaven and accept the sufficiency of Christ's atoning work for all sin – even when there is no opportunity to seek forgiveness. In doing this, we open up God's grace to those who are hurting. This step, alone, will help encourage clergy men and women to allow themselves the privilege to fail so that they too can accept God's restoring grace.

Our congregational and denominational systems must facilitate and encourage the men and women who give so much to be able to ask for help when needed. The barriers of judgmentalism, unforgiveness, pride, and social stigma that keep our leaders suffering in silence must come down. We must educate and advocate to save their lives, and offer them the hope that true Christian charity makes possible.

    Along with spiritual, and perhaps, material support, they may be in need of the very mental assistance to which their loved one failed to avail themselves.

5 Prayer for Pastors, Families and Churches

Heavenly Father,

I acknowledge you as the creator and giver of life. May your name be hallowed throughout the ages. You created men and women in your image and called us to live peacefully and lovingly together.

You commissioned us, as disciples of Jesus Christ, to share the good news of God's love and power to free us from the dominion of sin and death. You called us to be the church and to let our lights shine in the darkness of this world. Forgive us for walking in the darkness.

Give us the courage to repent of the way we do ministry. Loose our hearts from the fear and pride, and break the strongholds over minds that keep us locked into models of ministry and congregational practices that are unhealthy and destructive.

Grant us the wisdom and vision to chart a new path. Your Word reminds us that "there is a way that seems right to humans but in the end are the ways of death."
We are tired of death. Show us the path that leads to life for our pastors, our churches, our families, our children and our communities.

You are the God of all comfort and it is only in you that we find relief from the pain of losing those we love.

By the presence and power of your Spirit, wrap your loving arms around hurting families and churches who have lost pastors and leaders to the tragic end of suicide.

Be present with spouses who are left to pick up the psychological, emotional, and spiritual pieces left by loved ones who have come to such a tragic end.

Let our words as family and friends who stand with these families through all the stages of grief be life-giving words of comfort for the excruciating pain they are experiencing.

Manifest your assuring, sweet Spirit in times of worship and prayer, reminding the church of your promises of presence, guidance, and comfort through Christ our Lord.

Flood this nation with compassion for hurting leaders and the people they hurt. Inspire us to be generous and to share what we have with those in need.

Loving God ,

We know you are love, for your Word tells us so.

Let your love that bears all things, hopes all things, endures all things, and never fails, triumph over evil. Don't allow hopelessness, hatred, or darkness to prevail over the transforming power of your love.

Give us a love bold enough to tell each other the truth, and to walk with weaker brothers and sisters through dark times until the dawn of a new day breaks for them.

Help us to love ourselves enough to say no to ourselves and our desires that do not honor your name and our behaviors that hurt our neighbor – or ourselves.

Bind our hearts together in such a way that it hurts us to see each other in pain, and convict us when we try to turn a blind eye to the suffering of others.

Holy Spirit,

The Word of God tells us that you are the Helper… whom the Father will send in Christ's name, [and that You] will teach us all things, and bring to our remembrance all that Christ has said to us.

Break every stronghold of evil that draws us to self - destruction. Strengthen the men and women of God, cover them with your mercy, and keep them from evil. Keep them from yielding to the temptation to end their lives.

Strengthen and anoint your church to do authentic ministry and not race to be bigger and more powerful. Help us to seek to be faithful to the Great Commission, and to ministry to the least of these.

In Your power.

I give you thanks, Father, now for what you are about to do in this nation and across the world to bring life to your people and restore hope and purpose to your leaders.

I ask these things in the name of your Son, Jesus the Christ. For the praise and glory belong to you.

Amen.

Bibliography

Andrews, Mark. "Charismatic Church Network Leads Dies in Apparent Suicide." CharismaNews.com (August 27, 2014).

Barna, George. Revolution. Carol Stream IL: BarnaBooks, 2005.

Boys, Nigel. "T. D. Jakes Responds to Recent Pastor Suicides: Pastors Expected to do a lot and Expected to Survive on Crumbs," *AllChristianNews.Com.* (December 19, 2013).

Blair, Leonardo. "Pastor Who Committed Suicide Sunday Stopped Man from Taking Own Life Weeks Earlier…" *The Christian Post* (November 16, 2013).

Brogdon, Lewis. *Hope on the Brink: Understanding the Emergence of Nihilism in Black America.* Eugene: Cascade, 2013.

Blair, Leonardo. "Belief that Pastor who Killed Himself is Going to Hell is 'Ludicrous' and 'Unbiblical,' Say Dr. Richard Land, Pastor E. Dewey Smith," (November 14, 2013).

Chapell, Bryan. *The Hardest Sermons You'll Ever Have to Preach.* Grand Rapids: Zondervan, 2011.

Dodd, Brian. "Pastors and Suicide." *BrianDoddonLeadership.com.* (April 10, 2013).

Duin, Julia. *Quitting Church: Why the Faithful are Fleeing and What to do about it.* Grand Rapids: Baker, 2008.

George, Carl F. with Warren Bird. *How to Break Growth Barriers.* Grand Rapids: Baker Books, 1993.

Gray, Rudy. "Suicide: A Tragic Mistake." *Baptistcourier.com* (December 6 2012).

Gray, Rudy. "Pastoral Termination: An Epidemic?" *Baptistcourier.com* (January 3, 2013).

Krejcir, Richard J. "Statistics on Pastors: What is Going on with the Pastors in America." *The Schaeffer Institute* (2007).

LeClaire, Jennifer. "Why are so Many Pastors Committing Suicide?" *CharismaNews* (December 11, 2013).

London Jr., H. B. and Neil B. Wiseman. *Pastors at Greater Risk.* Ventura CA: Gospel Light Publications, 2003.

Olson, David T. *The American Church in Crisis.* Grand Rapids: Zondervan, 2008.

Rediger, G. Lloyd. *Clergy Killers.* Louisville: Westminster John Knox Press, 1997.

Sherman, Daniel. "Statistics on Pastor Burnout," *PastorBurnout.com* (publication date unknown).

Trip, Paul David. "Dealing with Depression in Ministry" *ChurchLeaders.com* (Date unknown).

Vitello, Paul. "Taking a Break from the Lord's Work," *The NewYorkTimes.com* (August 1 2010).

Warner, Greg. "Suicide: When Pastors' Silent Suffering Turns Tragic," *USAToday.com* (October 29, 2009).

Wellman, Jack. "Average Pastor Salaries in United States Churches," Patheos (December 15 2014).

Press Release: "Health, United States, 2013, Atlanta, Georgia: *The Center for Disease and Control* http://www.cdc.gov/media/releases/2014/p0514-prescription-drugs.html viewed May 14, 2014.

www.ingramcontent.com/pod-product-compliance
Lightning Source LLC
LaVergne TN
LVHW020934090426
835512LV00020B/3354